D1528133

by ISHMAEL REED

**NOVELS**

The Free-Lance Pallbearers

Yellow Back Radio Broke Down

Mumbo Jumbo

**POETRY**

Conjure

Chattanooga

# CHATTANOOGA

# Chattanooga

*Poems by* I S H M A E L  R E E D

R A N D O M  H O U S E  N E W  Y O R K

LIBRARY OF CONGRESS CATALOGING IN PUBLICATION DATA
Reed, Ishmael, 1938-
Chattanooga.
Poems.
I. Title.
PS3568.E365C5   813'.5'4   73-3992
ISBN 0-394-48778-8
MANUFACTURED IN THE UNITED STATES OF AMERICA

FIRST EDITION

"The Decade that Screamed," originally entitled "Rain
Rain on the Splintered Girl," was published in *Black
World* magazine September 1966

"Al Capone in Alaska" appeared in *Mark in Time,* Glide
Publications 1971

"Railroad Bill, A Conjure Man," "Haitians," "Skirt Dance"
and "Poison Light" appeared in *Yardbird Reader Vol. I,* a
publication of Yardbird Publishing Co. Inc. 1972

Photograph of General Grant and his officers on Lookout
Mountain, courtesy of the Tennessee State Library and Ar-
chives, Library Section.

Photograph of McLean House, courtesy of Virginia State
Library.

Dedicated to Sarah Fabio
Calvin Hernton and all the
other Chattanoogans who've
paid their Tennessee

An eyewitness later wrote that he accompanied some of his friends to the affair. He found the guests "to be composed of complicated ingredients." I do not suppose that the history of the world contains such a rare case of universal *concord* being the result of universal *discord*. The party was composed of 1st, Rebel and Union citizens; 2d, Rebel and Union soldiers; 3rd, Rebel and Union deserters; 4th, Rebel and Union spies; 5th, Rebel and Union bushwhackers.

Scarcely a harsh word was uttered during the whole night; all danced together as if nothing was wrong, and parted mutually the next morning, each party marching off separately.

Description of an all-night dance held near Chattanooga by a Mr. Reynolds, Feb. 17, 1863. Quoted in *The Chattanooga Country* by Govan and Livingood

# Contents

# CHATTANOOGA

## Chattanooga

### 1

Some say that Chattanooga is the
Old name for Lookout Mountain
To others it is an uncouth name
Used only by the uncivilised
Our a-historical period sees it
As merely a town in Tennessee
To old timers of the Volunteer State
Chattanooga is "The Pittsburgh of
The South"
According to the Cherokee
Chattanooga is a rock that
Comes to a point

They're all right
Chattanooga is something you
Can have anyway you want it
The summit of what you are
I've paid my fare on that
Mountain Incline #2, Chattanooga
I want my ride up
I want Chattanooga

### 2

Like Nickajack a plucky Blood
I've escaped my battle near
Clover Bottom, braved the
Jolly Roger raising pirates
Had my near miss at Moccasin Bend
To reach your summit so

Give into me Chattanooga
I've dodged the Grey Confederate sharpshooters
Escaped my brother's tomahawks with only
Some minor burns
Traversed a Chickamauga of my own
Making, so
You belong to me Chattanooga

3
I take your East Ninth Street to my
Heart, pay court on your Market
Street of rubboard players and organ
Grinders of Haitian colors rioting
And old Zip Coon Dancers
I want to hear Bessie Smith belt out
I'm wild about that thing in
Your Ivory Theatre
Chattanooga
Coca-Cola's homebase
City on my mind

4
My 6th grade teacher asked me to
Name the highest mountain in the world
I didn't even hesitate, "Lookout Mountain"
I shouted. They laughed
Eastern nitpickers, putting on the
Ritz laughed at my Chattanooga ways
Which means you're always up to it

To get to Chattanooga you must
Have your Tennessee
"She has as many lives as a
cat. As to killing her, even

( 4

the floods have failed
you may knock the breath out of
her that's all. She will re-
fill her lungs and draw
a longer breath than ever"
From a Knoxville editorial—
1870s


    5
Chattanooga is a woman to me too
I want to run my hands through her
Hair of New Jersey tea and redroot
Aint no harm in that
Be caressed and showered in
Her Ruby Falls
That's only natural
Heal myself in her
Minnehaha Springs
58 degrees F. all year
Around. Climb all over her
Ridges and hills
I wear a sign on my chest
"Chattanooga or bust"


    6
"HOLD CHATTANOOGA AT ALL
HAZARDS"—Grant to Thomas


When I tasted your big juicy
Black berries ignoring the rattle-
Snakes they said came to Cameron
Hill after the rain, I knew I
Had to have you Chattanooga
When I swam in Lincoln Park

Listening to Fats Domino sing
I found my thrill on Blueberry
Hill on the loudspeaker
I knew you were mine Chattanooga
Chattanooga whose Howard Negro
Tennyson and Dunbar
Whose Miller Bros. Department
Store cheated my Uncle out of
What was coming to him
A pension, he only had 6
Months to go
Chattanoooooooooooooooooooga
Chattanoooooooooooooooooooga

"WE WILL HOLD THE TOWN TILL
WE STARVE"—Thomas to Grant


   7
To get to Chattanooga you must
Go through your Tennessee
I've taken all the scotsboros
One state can dish out
Made Dr. Shockley's "Monkey Trials"
The laughing stock of the Nation
Capt. Marvel Dr. Sylvanias shazam
Scientists running from light-
ning, so
Open your borders. Tennessee
Hide your TVA
DeSota determined, this
Serpent handler is coming
Through

Are you ready Lookout Mountain?

"Give all of my Generals what he's
drinking," Lincoln said, when the
Potomac crowd called Grant a lush

   8
I'm going to strut all over your
Point like Old Sam Grant did
My belly full of good Tennessee
Whiskey, puffing on
A .05 cigar
The campaign for Chattanooga
Behind me
Breathing a spell
Ponying up for
Appomattox!

## Railroad Bill, A Conjure Man

A HooDoo Suite

Railroad Bill, a conjure man
Could change hisself to a tree
He could change hisself to a
Lake, a ram, he could be
What he wanted to be

When a man-hunt came he became
An old slave shouting boss
He went thataway. A toothless
Old slave standing next to a
Hog that laughed as they
Galloped away.
Would laugh as they galloped
Away

Railroad Bill was a conjure man
He could change hisself to a bird
He could change hisself to a brook
A hill he could be what he wanted
To be

One time old Bill changed hisself
To a dog and led a pack on his
Trail. He led the hounds around
And around. And laughed a-wagging
His tail. And laughed
A-wagging his tail

Morris Slater was from Escambia
County, he went to town a-toting
A rifle. When he left that
Day he was bounty.
Morris Slater was Railroad Bill
Morris Slater was Railroad Bill

Railroad Bill was an electrical
Man he could change hisself into
Watts. He could up his voltage
Whenever he pleased
He could, you bet he could
He could, you bet he could

Now look here boy hand over that
Gun, hand over it now not later
I needs my gun said Morris Slater
The man who was Railroad Bill
I'll shoot you dead you SOB
let me be whatever I please
The policeman persisted he just
Wouldn't listen and was buried the
Following eve. Was buried the
Following eve. Many dignitaries
Lots of speech-making.

Railroad Bill was a hunting man
Never had no trouble fetching game
He hid in the forest for those
Few years and lived like a natural
King. Whenever old Bill would
Need a new coat he'd sound out his
Friend the Panther. When Bill got
Tired of living off plants the

Farmers would give him some hens.
In swine-killing time the leavings of
Slaughter. They'd give Bill the
Leavings of slaughter. When he
needed love their fine Corinas
They'd lend old Bill their daughters

Railroad Bill was a conjure man he
Could change hisself to a song. He
Could change hisself to some blues
Some reds he could be what he wanted
To be

E. S. McMillan said he'd get old
Bill or turn in his silver star
Bill told the Sheriff you best
Leave me be said the outlaw from
Tombigbee. Leave me be warned
Bill in 1893

Down in Yellowhammer land
By the humming Chattahoochee
Where the cajun banjo pickers
Strum. In Keego, Volina, and
Astoreth they sing the song of
How come

Bill killed McMillan but wasn't
Willin rather reason than shoot
A villain. Rather reason than
Shoot McMillan

*"Railroad Bill was the worst old coon*
*Killed McMillan by the light of the*

*Moon*
*Was lookin for Railroad Bill*
*Was lookin for Railroad Bill"*

Railroad Bill was a gris-gris man
He could change hisself to a mask
A Ziba, a Zulu
A Zambia mask. A Zaramo
Doll as well
One with a necklace on it
A Zaramo doll made of wood

I'm bad, I'm bad said Leonard
McGowin. He'll be in hell and dead he
            Said in 1896
Shot old Bill at Tidmore's store
This was near Atmore that Bill was
            Killed in 1896.
He was buying candy for some children
Procuring sweets for the farmers' kids

Leonard McGowin and R. C. John as
Cowardly as they come. Sneaked up
On Bill while he wasn't lookin.
Ambushed old Railroad Bill
Ambushed the conjure man. Shot him
In the back. Blew his head off.

Well, lawmen came from miles around
All smiles the lawmen came.
They'd finally got rid of
Railroad Bill who could be what
He wanted to be

Wasn't so the old folks claimed
From their shacks in the Wawbeek
Wood. That aint our Bill in that
old coffin, that aint our man
You killed. Our Bill is in the
Dogwood flower and in the grain
We eat
See that livestock grazing there
That Bull is Railroad Bill
The mean one over there near the
Fence, that one is Railroad Bill

Now Hollywood they's doing old
Bill they hired a teacher from
Yale. To treat and script and
Strip old Bill, this classics
Professor from Yale.
He'll take old Bill the conjure
Man and give him a-na-ly-sis. He'll
Put old Bill on a leather couch
And find out why he did it.
Why he stole the caboose and
Avoided nooses why Bill raised so
Much sand.

He'll say Bill had a complex
He'll say it was all due to Bill's
Mother. He'll be playing the
Dozens on Bill, this
Professor from Yale

They'll make old Bill a neurotic
Case these tycoons of the silver
Screen. They'll take their cue

From the teacher from Yale they
Gave the pile of green
A bicycle-riding dude from Yale
Who set Bill for the screen
Who set Bill for the screen

They'll shoot Bill zoom Bill and
Pan old Bill until he looks plain
Sick. Just like they did old Nat
The fox and tried to do Malik
Just like they did Jack Johnson
Just like they did Jack Johnson

But it wont work what these hacks
Will do, these manicured hacks from
Malibu cause the people will see
That aint our Bill but a haint of
The silver screen. A disembodied
Wish of a Yalie's dream

Our Bill is where the camellia
Grows and by the waterfalls. He's
Sleeping in a hundred trees and in
A hundred skies. That cumulus
That just went by that's Bill's
Old smiling face. He's having a joke
On Hollywood
He's on the varmint's case.

Railroad Bill was a wizard. And
His final trick was tame. Wasn't
Nothing to become some celluloid
And do in all the frames.

Destroy the original copy
Pour chemicals on the master's
Copy

And how did he manage technology
And how did Bill get so modern?
He changed hisself to a production
Assistant and went to work with
The scissors.
While nobody looked he scissored
Old Bill he used the scissors.

Railroad Bill was a conjure man
He could change hisself to the end.
He could outwit the chase and throw
Off the scent he didn't care what
They sent. He didn't give a damn what
They sent.
Railroad Bill was a conjure man
Railroad Bill was a star he could change
Hisself to the sun, the moon
Railroad Bill was free
Railroad Bill was free

## The Kardek Method

No son, I dont wanta draw
I hung up my *Petro* in the Spring
of '68. Had got done with pick
ing notches; and what with the wing
ing and all, I ask you, was it
worth it?
So uncock your rod friend. Have
a sitdown.
While I stand back about 15 feet
think about some positive things. The
gals at the Road to Ruin Cabaret at the
end of the trail. The ranch in
Arizona you have your heart set
on.
Dont fret the blue rays emanating from
my fingers. They aint gonna cut you.
A-ha. Just as I thought. Your outside
aura looks a little grey. Your particles
cry the dull murmur of dying. I detect
a little green and red inside your
protecting sheet. You are here but
your ghost running cross a desert in a
greyhound. It bought a ticket to
No Place In Particular.
Swooooooooooooooooooosh!!
Yonder went the Combined Hand Pass
Feel Better?

## Haitians

**1**

Fell the leader and
Confuse the pack
Nature's way, this
Shaggy, limping buffalo
Is downed by
Fanged schemers with plenty
Of time, a dry, crawling,
Beach fooled a Chief Whale into
Thinking it was a sea

**2**

We too are taken in like
Fishbelly, Mississippi in
Paris, no sooner had he
Arrived but here they come
The jackals
Camping about his favorite
Cafés
Mooching off of him, the Blackamoors
Bearing tales about him on
A greenback pillow to the
Crew-cutted sheik
Remember?
*The Island of Hallucinations*

**3**

The prospect of Bird going
Tenor made saxophones leap
Like it was a Wall Street crash
Many hornmen were wiped out

**4**

You know, I used to be a
Hyena, many grins ago
Before my cabin door, this
Morning, the naked rooster
In the Georgia Sea Islands our
Brothers and Sisters have a
Cure for this mess. They
Let the sun infuse the print
    Me too

## Skirt Dance

i am to my honey what marijuana is
to tiajuana . the acapulco gold of her
secret harvest . up her lush coasts i
glide at midnite bringing a full boat .
(that's all the spanish i know.)

## Kali's Galaxy

My 200 inch eyes are trained
on you, my love spectroscope
Breaking down your wavelengths
With my oscillating ear
I have painted your
Portrait: ermine curled about
Yonder's glistening neck

They say you are light-years
Away, but they understand so
Little

You are so near to me
We collide
Our stars erupt into supernovae
An ecstatic cataclysm that
Amazes astronomers

I enter your Milky Way
Seeking out your suns
Absorbing your heat
Circumventing your orbs
Radiating your nights

Once inside your heavens
I hop from world to world
Until I can go no longer
And Z out in your dust
Your new constellation
Known for my shining process
And fish-tailed chariot

## Poison Light

FOR J. OVERSTREET

Last night
I played Kirk Douglas to
Your Burt Lancaster. Reflecting
20 years of tough guys I
Saw at the Plaza Theatre in
Buffalo, New York. I can
Roll an L like Bogart
You swagger like Wayne

Ours was a bad performance
The audience, our friends
Panned it. The box office
Hocked the producers

We must stop behaving like
The poison light we grew on

Ancient loas are stranded
They want artfare home
Our friends watch us. They
Want to hear what we say

Let's face it
My eye has come a long way
So has your tongue
They belong on a pyramid wall
Not in a slum
("Dead End"; 1937)

## The Decade that Screamed

the sun came up
the people yawned and stretched
in rat traps whipping mildewed cats,
pomaded and braced in gold bathrooms of
baroque toilet boxes,
from chairs with paws,
from snuff cases,
from the puzzlement of round square rooms
they poured into the streets,
yelling down phantom taxi cabs,
jostling old men
blowing their noses with tired flags

some came in steel rickshaws
some in buicks
some on weird pack animals
talking extinct words
(linguists bought them kool aid)
some popped gum
some were carried
some grumbled
some fondled pistols
others in trench coats jotted down names
for the state    took photos

babies set up tents
and auctioned off errant mothers
jive oatmeal was flung at finger-wagging humanists
who drew up their hind legs and split for the cafés
covering their faces with *Les Temps Moderne*
with grapefruit and cheeries

a famous editor was hanged on the spot for quoting
jefferson with almost no deliberation his credit cards
stamps line gauge correspondence and grey pages
slid towards the sewer

some sprinted
some bopped
some leaned on shaky lamp posts
others sat down
crossed their legs
and marveled
as the old men
talked of what was
talked of what is
talked of what is to come
talked crazy talk
toyed with their whiskers
threw difficult finger exercises at each other
(white lightning)

jumped like birds
jumped like lions
(yellow thunder)

a girl above   on a ledge toes over the edge
knees knocking teeth chattering

       JUMP JUMP JUMP (millions of hands megaphoning
          razored lips)

some danced
some sang
some vomited
stained themselves
pared fingernails

the moon came sick with old testament hang ups
people fought over exits
rain rain on the splintered girl
rain rain on deserted rickshaws, buicks

in certain rooms we ball our fists
"today in Cyprus, gunbattling"
in certain rooms we say   how awful
"today in Detroit, sniper fire"
rain rain on the splintered girl
rain rain on the baby auctioneers

## The Katskills Kiss Romance Goodbye

### 1

After twenty years of nods
He enters the new regime
The machine guns have been
Removed from the block
The women don't wear anything
You can see everything

### 2

Hendrick Hudson's Tavern
Has slipped beneath the
Freeway where holiday drivers
Rush as if they've seen the
Hessian Trooper seeking his
Head

### 3

They get their goosebumps at
The drive-in nowadays, where
The Lady in White at Raven
Rock is Bette Davis and
Burton apes Major André
Hanging before the Haunted
Bridge

### 4

A New England historian has
Proof that King George wasn't
So bad.
Gave in to every demand

Donated tea to the American needy
Yankees are just naturally jumpy

5

Where once stood madmen
Buttonholing you
Gentlemen think of Martinis
On the train to Mount Vernon

6

R.I.P. old Rip
Cuddle up in your Romance
Your dog Wolf is dead
Your crazy galigaskins out
Of style
Your cabbages have been canned
Your firelock isn't registered
Your nagging wife became a
Scientist, you were keeping
Her down

7

Go back to the Boarded Up
Alley and catch some more winks
Dreaming is still on the house

law isn't all
The drivers test
Says nothing about
dogs , but people
stop anyway

# Antigone, This Is It

FOR FRED

Whatever your name, whatever
Your beef, I read you like I
Read a book
You would gut a nursery
To make the papers, like
Medusa your Poster Queen
You murder children
With no father's consent

You map your treachery shrewdly,
A computer
Click clicking
As it tracks a ship
Headed for the Unknown
Making complex maneuvers
Before splashing down into
Mystery

Suppose everyone wanted it their
Way, traffic would be bottled up
The Horsemen couldn't come
There would be no beauty, no radio
No one could hear your monologues
Without drums or chorus
In which you are right
And others, shadows, snatching things

Fate, The Gods, A Jinx, The Ruling Class
Taboo, everything but you
All the while you so helpless
So charming, so innocent
Crossed your legs and the lawyer
Muttered, dropped your hankie
And the judges stuttered

You forgot one thing though, thief
Leaving a silver earring at the
Scene of a house you've pilfered
You will trip up somewhere
And the case will be closed

Standup Antigone,
The jury finds you guilty
Antigone, may the Eater
Of The Dead savor your heart
You wrong girl, you wrong
Antigone, you dead, wrong
Antigone, this is it

Your hair will turn white overnight

## And the Devil Sent a Ford Pinto Which She Also Routed

Sarah was banged &
Slammed & thrown &
Jostled , shook &
Shifted & ripped
& rumpled

D nex day she was on
D freeway

Tennesseeee women

   thoroughbreds

## Cuckoo

A cuckoo is a funny bird
Ridiculously masked he will
Tickle your tummy with
His quill
He will look like you
And be your brother

He will cheep your old favorites
At the drop of your dime

A cuckoo is a silly thing
Until he eliminates your offspring
And splits your ears with
His origin

## Rock Me, Baby

Turning Screw : In wave-guide
Technique an ad
Justing element in the form of
A rod whose depth of pene
Tration through the wall into
A wave-guide or cavity is ad-
Justable by rotating a screw

## Mystery 1st Lady

franklin pierce's wife never
came downstairs.   she never
came upstairs either.

## To a Daughter of Isaiah

I saw your drumming lover
On the tube last night
His wrists had been riveted
He made faces , like Jazz
Was a dentist
His gutbucket was
Straight from the Academy
That is , you couldn't
Grind to it
( Matthew Arnold, blowing
His nose )

He drummed , I summed
You up while helping white
Wine get better :
Your juicy Ethiopian art
Lips ( my , my )
Your moans . What moans !
Even the ceiling over the bed
Got hard

This happened way back in a book
You were my daughter of Isaiah
I was your flail and crook

## My Brothers

They come up here
Shit on my floor
Spill my liquor
Talk loud
Giggle about my books
Remove things from their
Natural places

They come up here
And crackle the snot-
Nosed sniggle about
My walk my ways my words

Signify about what is
Dear to me

My brothers
They come up here and
Hint at underhanded things
Look at me as if to
Invite me outside

My brothers
They come up here
And put me on the hot
Seat so I feel I am
Walking the last mile

My wrong , sorry, no
Manners brothers

I will invite them again
I must like it ?

You tell me

Contest ends at midnight

## The Vachel Lindsay Fault

All wines are
Not the same
Red, nor are
All Bloods

Nothing to
Brood about
But, nevertheless
A dud

## Back to Africa

A Tartar Wolf
Spider
Spinning
From the ceiling

Instead of
Squashing
You look
It up

## Swift, Tiny and Fine

He can climb vulgar
Like scooting up the
Side of a diamond
Discourse with a phoenix
Sail out to sea in a
Golden-brown doughnut
He can run a rodeo
With ants

This man
Can make the M in Mac
Donald's a rainbow
Transpose a sonata from
Fiddle to trumpet
Run out to the back yard
Pick a plum , eat that
Plum , run back
Sit down , cross his
Legs , smile
Then hear that sonata
Before it's tooted

Good

What the heck
I'm sick of Roller Derby champeens

A hummingbird standing still in mid air,
Robert Hayden is The Great Aware

( 40

# Crocidiles

A crocidile dont hunt
Him's victims
They hunts him
All he do is
Open he jaws

## Al Capone in Alaska

or
hoodoo ecology vs the judeo-
christian tendency to *let em*
have it!

The Eskimo hunts
the whale & each year
the whale flowers for the
Eskimo.
*This must be love baby!*
One receiving with respect
from a Giver who has
plenty.
There is no hatred here.
There is One Big Happy
Family here.

American & Canadian Christians
submachine gun the whales.
They gallantly sail out &
shoot them as if the Pacific
were a Chicago garage on
St. Valentine's day

# Visit to a Small College

you name your buildings after
john greenleaf whittier . you
left a great critic Nick Aaron
Ford waiting at the airport
for 3 hours . the room i
sleep in is scorching but
when i request an air
conditioner you think it
a joke .

" open the window, " you chuckle.

you invited me here but
don't have my books on your
list , or in your
bookstore .

i landed in your town
at 12 midnite & sarah
pointed to the blood on the
moon .

that will teach me to
mark my omens . believing
in future ones and up
dating old ones .
let's see
the president dropped the first
baseball of the season last yr .
what does that portend?

the last stanza of which is a
Russellian stanza named for its
best craftsman—Nipsey Russell

Many whiskey ads . More even than *The
New Yorker* . Not even the subtlety of
Coolidge , wearing Indian feathers but
Seagram's V.O. covers an entire page .
Does enamel prose drive its readers
to drink ? Living in New York ? Or
*Commentary*'s exchange of letters be
tween Podhoretz and Kazin ? Rapiers !
Stilettos ! Letter knives used to open
linen envelopes , 19 stories above the
upper West Side .

Well what about us and our razors ?
*The Rhythms , The Chicago Nation ,
The Crescent Moons , The Pythons or
The Berkeley Boppers* ? Man , we
Dukes and do we ? Muhammad Ali rum
blers ; Riders of the Purple Rage

Dear *Atlantic Monthly* Dec. 1970 .
Is Augustus still the Emperor ? Can
Rev. Billy Moyers dance on a dime ?
Is that Ralph Ellison in Frank Sin-

atra's raincoat or Floyd Patterson
lifting several White Hopes from
the canvas ? The album notes for
*Strangers in the Night* ?

Well what did I expect ? The multi
ple assassin theory of the *L.A.*
*Free Press* ? *E.V.O.*'s hepatitis
yellow ? The Dubious Achievements of
*Esquire* ? The Schwarz is Beautiful
school teacher over at *Evergreen*
clinging to her English text ?

You pays your dollar and you gets
Tabbed . Ah , that smooth velvet taste
We've come a long way from *Sneaky*
*Pete* , now hain't we ? You know
we is

Confidentially though ,
a young writer informed me that
this *Atlantic* issue made him
feel like Sugar Ray among the
Mormons . The black-as-Ham Utah
night when Sugar took off Gene
Fullmer's jaw . Never will for
get it. A left hook from out
of nowhere . And before his crafty
handlers could wise their boy to
the Sean O Casey shuffle and the
Mark Twain Possum , Fullmer had
done received his Baron Saturday
and was out cold on the floor.

" Why did they stop it ? I'm not hurt, the Kayoed Kid complained . But it was too late , the stadium was empty , and Sugar was on the train .

## The Last Week in 30

FOR  VICTOR  CRUZ  ON  D  MOON

5 before 2/22 i am
a magnified lizard in
a science fiction film. 1944
is when it was made; the
year ol men played volley
ball w/ children before add
ing them to the bones of
         europe

mother of dragons a swell
head said just as the ufo
carried him off .    right
on time too ; they signed his
happy papers d day befo . he
couldn/t keep his tongue
         still

i am spending my birthday in
a city built on junk left by
    a      glacier

a zoology professor/s wife jumped
off a bridge last week . that
fri he heard heavy breathing on
the other end of the line . the
news called it alienation

aint gon kill this cat . i
am moving into a new age . today
i broke the ice . my pulse begins to
move across a new world .

## Loup Garou Means Change Into

If Loup Garou means change into
When will I banish mine ?
I say , if Loup Garou means change
Into when will I shed mine ?
This eager Beast inside of me
Seems never satisfied

I was driving on the Nimitz wasn't
Paying it no mind
I was driving on the Nimitz wasn't
Paying it no mind
Before you could say "Mr. 5 by 5"
I was doin 99

My Cherokee is crazy
Can't drink no more than 4
My Cherokee is crazy
Can't stand no more than 4
By the time I had my 15th one
I was whooping across the floor
I was talking whiskey talking
I was whooping across the floor

Well, I whistled at a Gypsy who was reading at my cards
She was looking at my glad hand when something came
Across the yard started wafting across the kitchen
Started drifting in the room , the black went out her
Eyeballs a cat sprung cross her tomb
I couldn't know what happened til I looked behind the door
Where I saw her cold pale husband
WHO'S BEEN DEAD SINCE 44

They say if you get your 30
You can get your 35
Folks say if you get to 30
You can make it to 35
The only stipulation is you
Leave your Beast outside

Loup Garou the violent one
When will you lay off me
Loup Garou the Evil one
Release my heart my seed
Your storm has come too many times
And yanked me to your sea

I said please Mr. Loup Garou
When will you drop my goat
I said mercy Mr. Loup Garou
Please give me victory
I put out the beans that evening
Next morning I was free

If i had a nickel
For all the women who've
Rejected me in my life
I would be the head of the
World Bank with a flunkie
To hold my derby as i
Prepared to fly chartered
Jet to sign a check
Giving India a new lease
On life

If i had a nickel for
All the women who've loved
Me in my life i would be
The World Bank's assistant
Janitor and wouldn't need
To wear a derby
All i'd think about would
Be going home

## The Author Reflects on His 35th Birthday

35 ? I have been looking forward
To you for many years now
So much so that
I feel you and I are old
Friends and so on this day , 35
I propose a toast to
Me and You
35 ? From this day on
I swear before the bountiful
Osiris that
If I ever
If I EVER
Try to bring out the
Best in folks again I
Want somebody to take me
Outside and kick me up and
Down the sidewalk or
Sit me in a corner with a
Funnel on my head

Make me as hard as a rock
35 , like the fellow in
The story about the
Big one that got away
Let me laugh my head off
With Moby Dick as we reminisce
About them suckers who went
Down with the *Pequod*
35 ? I ain't been mean enough
Make me real real mean

Mean as old Marie rolling her eyes
Mean as the town Bessie sings about
"Where all the birds sing bass"

35 ? Make me Tennessee mean
Cobra mean
Cuckoo mean
Injun mean
Dracula mean
Beethovenian-brows mean
Miles Davis mean
Don't-offer-assistance-when
Quicksand-is-tugging-some-poor
Dope-under-mean
Pawnbroker mean
Pharaoh mean
That's it , 35
Make me Pharaoh mean
Mean as can be
Mean as the dickens
Meaner than mean

When I walk down the street
I want them to whisper
There goes Mr. Mean
"He's double mean
He even turned the skeletons
In his closet out into
The cold"

And 35 ?
Don't let me trust anybody
Over Reed but
Just in case
Put a tail on that
Negro too

February 22, 1973

Being a colored poet
Is like going over
Niagara Falls in a
Barrel

An 8 year old can do what
You do unaided

The barrel maker doesn't
Think you can cut it

The gawkers on the bridge
Hope you fall on your
Face

The tourist bus full of
Paying customers broke-down
Just out of Buffalo

Some would rather dig
The postcards than
Catch your act

A mile from the brink
It begins to storm

But what really hurts is
You're bigger than the
Barrel

# About the Author

ISHMAEL REED was born in Chattanooga, Tennessee. He grew
up in Buffalo, New York, learned to write in New York City
and wised-up in Berkeley, California. His first book of poetry,
*Conjure*, was published in 1972. His novels include *The
Free-Lance Pallbearers, Yellow Back Radio Broke Down* and
*Mumbo Jumbo*. The anthology he edited, *19 Necromancers
from Now*, is considered a breakthrough for independent
Afro-American writers of the 1960s. Reed was editor of
*Yardbird Reader*, Volume I. His poetry has been published in
many anthologies and magazines, including *Poetry of the
Negro, The New Black Poetry, The Friends Seminary Review,
Cricket, Poetry India, The Norton Anthology* and *Scholastic*
magazine.